Ralph Henry Shaw

Legend of the Trailing Arbutus and Other Poems

Ralph Henry Shaw

Legend of the Trailing Arbutus and Other Poems

ISBN/EAN: 9783337155957

Printed in Europe, USA, Canada, Australia, Japan

Cover: Foto ©Thomas Meinert / pixelio.de

More available books at **www.hansebooks.com**

Legend of the Trailing Arbutus

AND

OTHER POEMS,

BY

Ralph H. Shaw,

Author of " In Many Moods."

LOWELL, MASS.
1898.

CONTENTS.

LEGENDARY AND NARRATIVE.

LEGEND OF THE TRAILING ARBUTUS.

Do not reason, for you may
Reason all the charm away.

Many, many moons ago,
Lived an old man all alone;
In a wood that none may know,
By a stream as hard as stone.

Long and white was all his hair;
Heavy were the robes he wore;
Snow and ice were everywhere;
All the world to him was hoar.

Dark the night and wild the wind,
Wild the wind that roared amain,
When he searched the wood to find
Fuel for his fire in vain;

Sadly to his lodge returned;
Sat his last few embers by,
Bowed and prayed as low they burned
That with them he might not die.

3

"Mannaboosho! thou art good;
Mannaboosho! I am old;
Mannaboosho, give me wood,
Lest I perish from the cold!"

Thus he sat and thus he prayed,
When his door was blown aside,
And a maiden, unafraid,
Sought his presence, sunny-eyed.

In she came with dancing feet,
And she wore, to his delight,
Robes of ferns and grasses sweet,
Moccasins of lilies white.

Roses red were in her hair;
Willow-buds were in her hands;
Soon she gave the lodge the air,
Warmth and bloom of sunny lands.

"Welcome to my ashy fire!
Tell me, daughter, who you are,
That you have in such attire
Borne the biting cold so far.

"Sit beside me, very near,
Tell me all that I would know;
Of my wonders you shall hear,—
What is done by Manito."

"When I breathe," the maiden said,
  "Spring the flowers on the plains;
When I shake my curly head,
  Fall the warm and gentle rains."

"When I breathe," the old man said,
  "All the rivers cease to flow;
When I shake my hoary head,
  Falls the bleak and blinding snow."

"When I roam," the maiden said,
  "Light and lush the leaves come out;
Blithe the birds sing overhead;
  All the rivers laugh and shout."

"When I roam," the old man said,
  "Blow the leaves about the sky;
Like an arrow overhead,
  All the wild-geese from me fly."

While they talked the lodge grew warm;
  Wide awake he could not keep;
Soon he stretched his heavy form,
  Bowed his head, and fell asleep.

On the lodge the sunshine fell;
  O'er the lodge the bluebird cheeped;
Soon the springs began to well,
  Soon the river laughed and leaped.

Low the maiden as he lay
　　Bent and breathed his body o'er;
Saw it sink and fall away,
　　Melt from out the robes he wore;

Saw the robes—with keen delight—
　　Turn to leaves of living green;
Then she knelt, and flowers white
　　Fondly hid the leaves between.

"Precious flowers, unto you,
　　Give I all my purity;
Who would pick you, so must do
　　Humbly and on bended knee."

This she said, and moved away
　　Through the woods, by hill and dell:
Lo! the arbutus to-day
　　Trails where'er her footsteps fell.

[I came across this legend in a newspaper abstract of a paper read by the Hon. C. E. Belknap of Michigan, before the American Folklore Society, at a meeting held in Washington, D. C. This gentleman said: "On the south shore of Lake Superior, in the vicinity of the Pictured Rocks, grows to perfection that dearest and sweetest of all wild flowers, the arbutus. The plant that the most skilful florist, the plant that the tender, loving touch of woman even, cannot cause to grow in hot-house or garden. And this is the legend as told me of the origin or creation of the arbutus." Longfellow in "Hiawatha" has presented another version of this Chippewa legend. In his version there is reference to the overcoming of Winter by Spring, not to the creation of the arbutus, of which nothing is said. The only flower mentioned is the spring-beauty, or *Claytonia Virginica*, called by the Chippewas *Miskodeed*. The legend bears strong resemblance to the Passamaquoddy legend of the conflict between Heat and Cold, or Spring and Winter. Indeed, Mr. Leland is of the opinion that the Passamaquoddy is a "completer form" of the Chippewa.]

6

THE GIFT OF KATAHDIN.

AN ALGONQUIN LEGEND.

Long ago, an Indian maiden,
On Katahdin, said:
"Would I that I had a husband —
Better to be wed!"

And beholding how Katahdin
Rose in majesty:
"O, that human were Katahdin,
And would marry me!"

Then she wandered on and upward,
And was seen no more
Till had passed the circling seasons
Thrice Katahdin o'er;

When she came among her people,
Where she yet was known,
With a little child, but listen!
One whose brows were stone.

Now the Spirit of Katahdin
Had this maiden wed,
And when she would seek her people,
"Go in peace," he said;

"Go, and tell them they are never
To inquire of thee
Who the father of thy child is —
All his brows may see.

"He will have the god-like power
To direct and lead,
To provide for all his people,
Great in thought and deed;

"But to them most dire ever
Shall be all events,
If they grieve thee with rude questions,
With impertinence.

"They will surely know his father,
When his brows they see;
So, for asking who his father,
There no need will be."

Now, when she had sought her people,
They were straightway told
Not to ask the idle question,
But their peace to hold.

Soon they saw the child had powers
Far beyond their head;
That he was a great magician,
All the wise men said;

For if he but aimed his finger,
Moose and wild duck fell,
And through him, whate'er the season,
Lived his people well.

But, alas! for all their feasting,
They would ask her what
They had been forbade to ask her;
Said they this and that;

Till the maiden, angered hearing
How their tongues would run,
Answered: "Truly, you are nowise
Worthy of my son.

"Fools, who kill yourselves by folly;
Mud-wasps,—worse than fools,—
Stinging fingers that would save you
From the fatal pools,—

"Why insist that I should tell you
What you have been told?
Surely, you must know his father,
Who his brows behold.

"By the Spirit of Katahdin
Came this child to be;
But it shall be to your sorrow
That you questioned me.

"Hence, this child no more shall serve you;
You, yourselves may feed;
Many hence will be your hardships,
Sore will be your need."

Then she took the child and bore him
Through the woods away,
And his people for their folly
Weakened day by day.

Truly, it would have been better,
In the days of old,
Had those people had the wisdom
Their poor tongues to hold.

THE LEGEND OF INDIAN CORN.

(ALGONQUIN.)

N' Karnayoo.

Long ago, when all was new,
While the Indians yet were few,
There was one who dwelt alone ;
Fire to him was all unknown,
And he lived on barks and roots,
Nuts and other forest fruits.

He grew lonesome, it is said,
Weary of the life he led ;
Barks and roots and nuts at length
Failed to give him needful strength.
Sick of all, one quiet day,
Sleeping in the sun he lay.

When he woke he saw in fear
Something standing strangely near ;
But his fear was gone when he
Saw through half the mystery,—
That the something was a fair,
Beauteous girl, with long, light hair.

Oft as he, whose heart was fired,
Would approach her, she retired,
Till he told her, in a song,
That he had been lonely long,
And besought her o'er and o'er
To be with him evermore.

Then she told him if he would
Do her bidding as he should,
Do it well and faithfully,
She would always with him be;
And she looked so fair and good,
That he promised her he would.

So she led him by the hand
To a dry yet grassy land;
Bade him two long splinters get,
Dry as they had ne'er been wet,
Hold them firmly, bending low,
Rub them fast together, so.

This he did; a spark flew out,
Set on fire the grass about.
Fast the fire, reaching round,
Wrought a black patch on the ground;
When in wonder, much amazed,
He upon the stranger gazed.

Then she said, "When sets the sun
And the night comes sad and dun,
Take me by my long, light hair,
And, though I may seem too fair,
Drag me o'er the singèd ground,
Back and forward and around."

This he was full loth to do,
And she bade him once anew,
Saying, where he dragged her so,
Something like to grass would grow,
Which when fit for use would bear,
Like a tuft, her own light hair.

So his promise to obey
Well he kept; and to this day,
When they see the silken hair
On the cornstalk,— long and fair,—
Know the Indians they are not
By the wondrous one forgot.

GLOOSKAP AND MALSUM.

AN ALGONQUIN LEGEND.

GLOOSKAP, *the Good Principle.*
MALSUM, (*the wolf*) *the Evil Principle.*
KWAH-BEET-A-SIS, *the Beaver.*
KO-KO-KHAS, *the Owl.*

I.

MALSUM.

How hateful has the sight of Glooskap grown
To me who am his brother; not alone
Because he walks erect and is deemed fair,
But also and especially because
The voice of nature, present everywhere,
Does magnify his goodness without pause !
Here in this sunny, flower-sprinkled wood,
Have I not heard this morning every air
Sing, "Glooskap ! Glooskap ! greatly wise and good !"
As I have heard the falling waters sing
When in their haunts I have been wandering ?
I have had visions: even now I see
How many hence his worshippers will be —

Will be, unless I steal his life away,
And to do that shall be my aim to-day.
His life is charmed; but, even like my own,
It has its bane, which shall to me be known.

(*Enter Glooskap.*)

MALSUM.

Twin-brother Glooskap, every wind that blows,
And rill that falls and pebbly brook that flows,
And every bird that sings by day or night,
All vocal things in shadow and in light,
Extol thy name, as every mortal should ;
All nature holds thee greatly wise and good.
Our lives are charmed. I would they were likewise,
For if they were I might be more like thee.
Our lives are charmed. Herein the secret lies :
Two things alone can fatal to them be.
Confide to me what can be so to thine,
And thou shalt know what can be so to mine !
Am I as safe, secure as thou in whom
All nature joys as now in sun and bloom?

GLOOSKAP.

Malsum, thy words are pleasant to my ear ;
But leave me by myself a moment here !

(*Exit Malsum.*)

GLOOSKAP.

How cunning would my brother Malsum be,
Who sweetens speech with insincerity !
Well I remember our prenatal life,
And how he chose — already fond of strife —
To seek this world awry and, bursting through
His mother's side, his suffering mother slew.
Shall I impart to him what is my bane,
Knowledge of that which is his own to gain?
Ah! can it be that Malsum does not know
'T is not in me that nature does rejoice
From morn to morn with many-tonèd voice,
With all her tongues throughout this leafy wood,
With all her tongues wherever he may go;
But simply in the principle of good,
Most active in my being? Evil one!
I must not by his cunning be outdone.
That which can do me harm I will not tell,
But that to which I am invulnerable.

(Enter Malsum.)

GLOOSKAP.

Malsum, I can by nothing else be slain
Than an owl's feather. What is thy sole bane?

MALSUM.

My brother, my twin-brother Glooskap, I
Am not so safe; but I can only die
Struck by a fern-root. Many a one is nigh,
And so at peace I neither walk nor lie.

(Exeunt.)

16

II

MALSUM.

I have been tempted, wandering through this wood,
Where all the leaves sing, "Glooskap, great and
     good,"
And all the airs that whisper in my ear
So breathe his name that he seems present here,
To take my bow and slay dull Ko-ko-khas;
For one of all the feathers that he has,
Unwitting bird, will serve to put an end
To that charmed life that does but me offend.
Ah, Ko-ko-khas! the best of birds art thou,
Though ne'er before so much esteemed as now;
Stir not, but mope! thou hast an easy bough;
Mope, Ko-ko-khas! the sun that blinds thine eye
No more shall blind it; sweet it is to die.
                  (*Shoots the Owl.*)

How little are the great! for Glooskap saith
That even to him a feather's touch is death,
This feather's touch, which shall be light as breath.
Ah, Ko-ko-khas! thy wisdom seemeth less :
Thou didst not know what thou didst long possess,—
Cure for the first and chiefest wretchedness.
Oh, what a calm has fallen o'er this wood,
Where now the leaves lisp, "Glooskap, great and
     good,"

And not a frond is shaken in such wise
That it escapes the beam that on it lies!
In this deep calm — which hideous is to me,
Since, vexed by hatred, calm I cannot be —
I may find Glooskap, as I would, asleep;
So let me seek him, and my purpose keep!

(*Finds Glooskap sleeping and touches him with
the feather.*)

GLOOSKAP (RISING).

Malsum, thine act doth only anger me;
No good at all but evil lives in thee.
Depart! for I thy brotherhood disown.
Never by thee shall my sole bane be known.

(*Exit Malsum.*)

GLOOSKAP.

Now comes a struggle 'twixt the good and ill,
And both are strong: but one shall have its will.
Here by this brook let me resume my rest,
And ponder what behooveth Glooskap best!
Was I not false to Malsum, so that he
For my defect can look in scorn on me?
It were not well — his questioning to hush —
To say my bane is but a flowering rush.

(*Exit Glooskap.*)

18

III.

KWAH-BEET-A-SIS.

Malsum, thou hast by Glooskap been deceived ;
For Glooskap thou hast overmuch believed ;
And I, who hide among the reeds, have heard
What I can tell thee, Malsum, word for word ;
But why should I, who have to work so hard,
Advantage any without some reward?

MALSUM.

Whate'er thou wishest shall be given thee,
If thou wilt tell what can advantage me ;
So tell it quickly, and no mumbler be !

KWAH-BEET-A-SIS.

Well, Malsum, hid among the reeds to-day,
I heard thy brother, thy twin-brother, say :
"Was I not false to Malsum, so that he
For my defect can look in scorn on me?
It were not well—his questioning to hush —
To say my bane is but a flowering rush."
Now, Malsum, for this service rendered thee
So truly and with such alacrity,
I—who have toiled in water and in mud
E'er since creation spread its earliest flood,
Ambitious from my oozy haunts to rise,
As is a water-lily for the skies —
Ask thee for wings which Glooskap me denies.

O most ungainly of ungainly things!
Oh, get thee hence! how wouldst thou look with
    wings?
    (*Exeunt; Kwah-beet-a-sis seeking Glooskap.*)

IV.

KWAH-BEET-A-SIS.

Glooskap, arise! my presence tolerate!
For I have much of moment to relate.
Give ear to me, if thou naught else canst give,
And let me hence thy humblest servant live!
Here by this brook, among the reeds, to-day,
When I was more than ever discontent,
My lot being worse than unjust punishment,
I heard thee, Glooskap, meditating say:
"Was I not false to Malsum, so that he
For my defect can look in scorn on me?
It were not well — his questioning to hush —
To say my bane is but a flowering rush."
And this I told to Malsum, for my head
Was by my hope of gain bewilderèd.
But my reward was Malsum's treachery:
He promised much and but derided me.
I come to make the best amends, and be
For my disgraceful act amerced of thee.

GLOOSKAP.

Kwah-beet-a-sis, thou art beneath contempt,
As infamous as awkward and unkempt,
Who, liking not the water and the mire
Wherein thou livest,— for thou dost aspire,—
Of evil askest favor and in league
With evil joinest in most foul intrigue.
Thou dost aspire, but thou hast done thy worst.
Look thou to Malsum, whom thou sought'st at first,
And be with Malsum henceforth doubly curst!

(Exit Kwah-beet-a-sis.)

GLOOSKAP.

Give me thy root, O Fern! give it, I pray!—
Glooskap must act as Malsum acts, to-day :
Advance,— recede,— seek cover,— watch,— way-
    lay,—
Pursue,— and when the time is opportune
For striking, strike. Oh, may that time be soon!
For Malsum must be stricken of this root,
And with his life be ended his pursuit,—
Unwearying destruction of the good.
Awake, O Airs! in every leafy wood,
Awake, O Brooks! and sing in Malsum's ear
The happy songs that he is pained to hear!
And shine, O Sun! on every hill and vale,
On every slope, in every secret dale,
So that his eye shall sicken of the sight,—

Himself the one great shadow in the light!
But I must seek him. First to yonder wood
Of thickest pines, a darksome solitude,
But not too dark for Malsum's mind, let me
Direct my steps! for Malsum there may be,
Since he likes darkness who lives cowardly.

(Enters the wood.)

Shall I go farther? who, ah! who is that
That sitteth yonder, turning in the hand
A flowering rush and looking down thereat?
'T is Malsum! ah! my life cannot withstand
One touch of what he holds. Let me be swift!
And suddenly as sometimes through a rift
Descends the sun, as noiselessly withal,
Let me upon mine adversary fall
And strike him with this weapon!

(Approaches Malsum from the rear and strikes him with the fern-root.)

It is done!
Shine through these damp and darksome pines,
        O Sun!
In every nook and corner of the earth!
To all things give the brightness of new birth!
And sing, O Airs! in every leafy wood:
O'ercome has been the evil by the good!

"THE MOURNFUL MYSTERY OF THE PAR-
TRIDGE-WITCH;

Setting Forth How a Young Man Died From Love."

AN ALGONQUIN LEGEND.

N'Karnayoo.

Two companions, happy brothers,
  Hunted once, in days of old,
Through the autumn long and chilly,
  Through the winter long and cold,
Till the winds of March returning
  Through the woods began to blow,
Where the wild Penobscot rises,
  Down its rocky way to flow.

Then they found their worn-out garments
  Needed what they could not do,
For they had not woman's fingers
  That can make an old thing new;
So they turned their faces homeward,
  And the younger ran ahead,
For in every homely duty
  It was he that always led.

23

Great was his surprise at finding,
  When he entered at the door,
That a woman, very busy,
  Had been at the lodge before;
Garments had been nicely mended,
  Mats been swept and shaken clean,
And a cheerful pot was boiling,
  Though no one about was seen.

Said he nothing to his brother,
  And returning the next day
Found the lodge again in order,
  And again did nothing say;
But when hunting on the morrow,
  Watched in hiding near the door,
And beheld a graceful maiden
  Come and pass the threshold o'er.

Then he entered, stepping softly,
  And she trembled, much alarmed;
But his pleasant words of welcome
  Soon her heaving bosom calmed;
And they sported long together,
  Here and there the pines among,—
Sported happily like children,
  For indeed they both were young.

When the sun was nigh to sinking
    And the shadows all were long,
Said the maiden : "I must leave you,
    (There's an end to every song)
For I hear your brother coming,
    And your brother much I fear;
But I will return to-morrow.
    Look for me to-morrow here!"

So she went, and on the morrow
    Came again with laughing face;
And they frolicked in the woodland
    Till the day had run its race,—
In the sunshine and the shadow
    Till the parting hour came,
When he sighed :   "Oh, do not leave me!
    Here abide, and be the same!"

But, receding, she made answer:
    "Tell your brother, nothing loth,
What has happened, and it may be
    I will come and serve you both."
Then, as down the far horizon,
    Out of sight the great sun fell,
She departed from his vision —
    Whither, he could scarcely tell.

When she reached the lodge next morning,
   It was her delight to hear
Words of welcome from the elder,
   Whom she did no longer fear. . . .
Chores were done as if by magic
   As she quickly moved about,
Till the elder to the father
   Let the long-kept secret out.

Spake the father very angry:
   "All my life have I feared this;
Verily, this charming creature
   Is a female Mikumwess;
Very cunning, very artful,
   Working evil here and there;
Witch or devil, call her either;
   'T is of her you should beware."

And he spake so much in earnest
   That the brothers were afraid
They had set their lives in danger,
   She so well could ply her trade;
So the elder, closely followed
   By the younger all about,
Bound to slay her, in obedience
   To the father, started out;

Sought her in the bosky woodland,
  Sought her by the brawling stream,
With as little self-direction
  As one wanders in a dream,
Till at last he found her bathing,
  Adding graces to a rill,
When espying him she startled
  And ran up a little hill.

Then he shot his ready arrow,
  And beheld, the wise men say,
But a scattering of feathers
  And a partridge fly away;
Still believing he had slain her,
  To the father he returned,
Straightway followed by the younger
  In whose bosom something yearned.

"It is well and it was well done,"
  The delighted father said,
"Much I know of female devils
  That will turn a young man's head;"
But the younger, unforgetful,
  Longed to see her face once more,
Sought and found her, and she met him,
  Full of kindness as before.

"Truly, 't was not at my bidding
    That my brother shot at you;
Let us be the friends we have been,
    All our woodland sports renew!"
"Well I know 't was at your father's;
    But it is the wisest way
Not to mind the past or future
    But the things that are to-day."

So, forgetting all their troubles,
    They made merry till the sun,
Resting on a far-off hill-top,
    Told them that the day was done;
When she said : "You must be going;
    But whene'er you long for me,
Seek me in this piny woodland;
    I shall here in waiting be.

"And remember what I tell you,—
    Since I tell it for your sake,—
Do not marry any other,
    Deadly would be such mistake.
Though I am a witch or devil
    If your father you believe,
I am not so cunning, artful,
    As a loved one to deceive."

This he heard, but not astonished;
  For he had begun to see
She was not like other women,
  But a deeper mystery;
And, though still his heart was beating
  With a love for her untold,
He made light of all her bidding,
  For he waxed both brave and bold;

And returning to his father,
  Heard his father sternly say:
"I have found for you a woman;
  Let the wedding be to-day!"
And he answered: "Let it be so!
  Since you choose that I shall wed:"
And the bride came quickly forward,
  And was straightway to him led.

Four long days they danced and feasted,
  Danced and feasted o'er and o'er;
But upon the fourth he uttered,—
  "I can dance and feast no more."
Then he laid him on a bear-skin,
  Seized by sickness, heart and head,
And when last the bride looked on him
  He was lying coldly dead.

Well the father knew the sickness ;
  But of it he never spake.

Soon his native wood was gruesome,—
  Every bramble, bush and brake ;
There were voices in its shadows
  That disturbed him night and day,
And he moved with all his people
  Far and farther still away.

[Charles Godfrey Leland, in commenting on this legend,
says: "This strange story recalls the Undine of la Motte
Fouqué. There is in it an element of mystery and destiny,
equal in every way to anything in German literature. The
family secret, touched on but never explained, which ends
in such a death, is, speaking from an artistic point of view,
very skilfully managed. It must be borne in mind that in
this, as in most of these (Algonquin) tales, there are asso-
ciations and chords which make as gold to an Indian that
which is only copper, or at best silver, to the civilized
reader of my translations.

"There is a characteristic feature in this story superior
to anything in Undine. It is the growth in the hero, when
he knows the worst to come, of that will, or stoicism, or
complete indifference to fate, which the Indians regard as
equivalent to attaining *m'téoulin*, or magic power. When a
man has in him such courage that nothing earthly can do
more than increase it, he has attained to what is in one sense
at least *Nirvana*. From an Algonquin point of view the
plot is perfect. I have given this story accurately as it was
told to me by Tomah Josephs, a Passamaquoddy Indian."]

THE CRY OF THE LOON.

How weird to you, in the light of the moon,
My little lads, is the cry of the loon,
When quiet lies over valley and hill,
And wood and mere are uncannily still!
But, listen, lads, there is something to know,—
A tale oft-told in an age long ago,
By wigwam fires that no torch can renew,—
A tale that ends with the saying: "Kwemoo
El-komik-too-ajul Gloocapal"—
The loon is calling on Glooskap.

Glooskap was God to the untutored mind
Lit by the lights that in nature we find,
That heard this tale and believed it throughout
As something 't were sacrilegious to doubt;
And once he saw, from the marge of a lake,
A flock of loons o'er the wide water make
Thrice for the land as in circles they flew.
So runs the tale with the saying: "Kwemoo
El-komik-too-ajul Gloocapal"—
The loon is calling on Glooskap.

Then up the marge, in a line from the lake,
He saw them come, who approached him and spake:
"Be near to us who have sought after thee!
Be near to us who thy servants would be!"
Nodding he said: "I will teach one and all
What I shall know as a prayerful call."
And so he taught what is heard, lads, by you;
And hence arose that old saying: "Kwemoo
El-komik-too-ajul Gloocapal"—
The loon is calling on Glooskap.

Glooskap was good; and methinks you will find,
If you, my lads, keep this legend in mind,
That far-off cry, which is only a prayer,
Will sound less weird in the pale, moony air,
Or make less wild and less gruesome the night
When all is still over valley and hight.
But, howsoe'er it may be, lads, with you,
Whene'er you hear that long cry say: "Kwemoo
El-komik-too-ajul Gloocapal"—
The loon is calling on Glooskap.

WEELAHKA.

Many, many years ago,
From the valley far below,
Came an Indian maiden here,
Saying, sad, with many a tear,
"Could I sing, then I would be
Dear to one who's dear to me.

"He is fond of brooks and birds;
He interprets all their words;
Stops, and listens to their song;
In his rapture, tarries long;—
O, if I could sing as they,
He would wed me on this day!"

Now the mountain Spirit heard
Every murmur, every word,
Of this maiden young and fair,
Heavy-hearted, full of care;
Saw the beauty in her face,
All her sweetness, all her grace.

33

"I will give to her a voice
That shall make all hearts rejoice;
But she must forever bide,
Changed in body, at my side."
This above her bending head
To himself the Spirit said.

Soon she found the turf whereon
She had thrown herself was gone;
Soon she found she ceased to sigh,
Wildly laughed, she knew not why,
And in happy, careless mood
Charmed with song the listening wood.

This is how there came to be
On the side of Ossipee,
Said the wise men long ago,
What we as Weelahka know.
Brook or spirit, to this day
It has stolen hearts away.

THE LEGEND OF THE FRINGED GENTIAN.

Distant from her hidden home,
Cavern deep with crystal dome,

On a bright, autumnal day,
Wandered once a tiny fay;

Fearing naught, till by and by
Rose a cloud that, dark and high,

Threatened, in its fall, to mar
Wings so fine as fairies' are.

Welladay!--She looked in vain
For some shelter from the rain.

Hers was but a narrow view;
What was she, poor thing, to do?

Turned she here and turned she there;
Naught to climb was anywhere,

Save a thistle, tall and straight,
Which she gave her airy weight.

Lo! beside a little brook,
Wimpling through its leafy nook,

Saw she now a flower hold
To the cloud its cup of gold.

Happy fay! she, like a ray,
Lit upon it, and straightway,

Close within its ample cup,
Bade its petals fold her up.

Fast and faster fell the rain;
Beat upon the flower in vain;

Close together to the last
Held the flower its petals fast.

When the vicious rain was o'er
And the sun came out once more,

Raised the fay — who well could thank—
Her true flower to royal rank;

Robing it, that all might see,
None mistake, its high degree,

In the bluest of the blue
That a mortal ever knew.

THE CHALLENGE AND THE ANSWER.
1621.

While the early bluebirds sing
In the Plymouth woods of spring;

While beneath a rosy ray
Melts the ice in Plymouth bay,

And the Pilgrim offers praise
For the promised better days,—

Like an arrow from the sky,
All so sudden to the eye,

Lights a brave in Plymouth town,
Where he throws a quiver down,

Turns him quickly thereupon,
And is in a moment gone.

Holds the quiver, it is found,
Arrows with a snake-skin bound,

37

Sent to little Plymouth thus
By the fierce Canonicus,

As a token to all eyes
That he hates and he defies.

Ere the pleasant light of day
Fades from peaceful Plymouth bay,

Back to him of dark intent,
Powder-stuffed, the skin is sent,

For the wisdom is to show
Heart of courage to the foe;

But in fear the palisade
Stouter far by night is made,

And a watch as ne'er before
Set the homes of Plymouth o'er.

LYRICAL.

AGAIN.

Again to these familiar hills
  My love has come with me,
And like a light and careless girl
  She bears me company.
Again for her these wildwoods wave,
  These winding waters pour;
Again I live, in all I feel,
  Our first, sweet summer o'er.

Again she wears the jaunty cap
  She would not wear in town,
And tied with silken bows she lets
  Her braided tresses down.
For years a mother, still her face
  Its early freshness wears.
Ah! who would say that she had borne
  A hundred household cares?

Again I wait to raise the boughs
    Above her bending head,
As when amid the tangled wood
    Her early steps I led;
Again to help her climb the steep,
    The rough and rugged way,
As when a bashful lad I longed
    My hand in hers to lay.

Oh, may she know that still to me,
    Among these summer hills,
She 's praised by all their whispering airs
    And all their singing rills!
And may I many summers live
    Our first, sweet summer o'er,
Ere light among these hills shall be
    Her step and mine no more!

THE WAKENING.

I rise from my couch and far away
I see the light of the dawning day.

There 's not a whisper about the hill;
All leaves save the poplar leaves are still.

If I rouse my love who slumbers near,
Will her looks be looks of sudden fear?

I will touch her hand: she would not miss
The tender charm of an hour like this.

And soft and light as the stir I see
In the poplar leaves my touch shall be,

So that she may from her slumber rise
As if the day had unsealed her eyes.

THE WOOD-THRUSH.

My absent dear, my darling,
　The wood-thrush kens, I trow,
The feeling that is in my heart,
　Which very few may know.

For Oh! my dear, my darling,
　It sings a sadder song
Than I have heard it sing before
　For many a summer long.

My absent dear, my darling,
　My loneliness has found
A singer in this gray-mossed wood
　Whose shadows deepen round.

But oh! my dear, my darling,
　The singer sings in vain;
For thou—thou dost not hear the song,
　And lonely I remain.

WILLETTE.

That little, witching, mountaineer,
  With what delight I met her!
Her looks, her ways, they make her dear—
  I never shall forget her.

I see her now, though far away,
  As last among the mountains,—
As sunny as their sunny day,
  As sportive as their fountains,

In sweet unconsciousness of all
  The charms that grace her childhood,
Receiving, where her footsteps fall,
  The homage of the wildwood.

The ferns that nod as she goes by,
  The leaves that clap above her,
Are not less pleased, methinks, than I,
  Because, methinks, they love her.

God bless her, little mountaineer,
  And may she keep forever
That spirit that does most endear
  And is forgotten never!

OH, TELL ME!

I catch you, hold you, dearest dear,
  A captive on my knee;
I catch you, hold you, dearest dear,
  Now tell it all to me!
Oh, tell me how the sunbeams fall,
  The flowers bloom, to-day,
  In that world of yours,
  Where the Spring endures
  And all is light and gay,
          My dear,
  And all is light and gay!

Oh, sweet to me your laughing glee,
  Your rippling, gurgling voice!
Oh, sweet to me your laughing glee!
  I hear it and rejoice.
Oh, tell me if you caught its tones
  From some melodious stream
  In that world of yours,
  Where the Spring endures
  And life is like a dream,
          My dear,
  And life is like a dream'!

44

How beautiful your deep blue eyes!
  How soft their witchery!
How beautiful your deep blue eyes,
  That work their spell on me!
Oh, tell me if you caught their charm
  From that cerulean sky
  In that world of yours
  Where the Spring endures;
  And then I 'll say,—Goodbye,
              My dear,
  And then I 'll say,—Goodbye!

IN THE SHADOW.

The day is dark and dull;
  The clouds are thick and low;
With sighs and sobs among the leaves
  The wet winds come and go.

But 't is the thought of one
  Whose prattle charmed my ear,
That to my heart its sadness gives
  And to my eye its tear.

I kissed her forehead fair;
  I kissed her fingers cold;
And then a bit of pussy-willow
  I gave to her to hold.

She wanders far away
  In some sunshiny land,
And there are flowers after flowers
  Inviting to her hand.

She looks on them with wonder —
  O God! am I to find
She bears the bit of pussy-willow
  And leaves the flowers behind?

46

LET 'S GO A-MAYING.

Sin no more, as we have done, by staying;
But, my Corinna, come, let 's go a-Maying.
* * * * * *
A deal of youth, ere this, is come
Back, and with white-thorn laden home.
* * * * * * *
Yet we 're not a-Maying.
—*Robert Herrick*, 1594-1674.

Oh, be not like Corinna,
  Who slept the morn away!
But rise, and be a winner
  Of flowers, born of May,
  While yet 't is early day—
    'T is early day.

Unlike her patient lover,
  I have not time to wait;
I cannot sing twice over
  My verses at your gate;
  So rise, or else be late—
    Or else be late.

The wings of Time beat faster,
  Or seem to, since the day
When he—sweet lyric master—
  Bade her not long delay.
  So come, let 's be away—
    Let 's be away.

47

The day is not all ours
  Sweet pleasure to pursue;
So come, let 's gather flowers,
  And be content with few.
  I 'll give all mine to you —
    All mine to you.

ASSOCIATION.

Last year, when I was here before,
And looked this quiet landscape o'er,
Through which without a murmur pour
    The waters of the Concord,
I did not say what now I say —
How beautiful what I survey!
How lovely as they wind away,
    The waters of the Concord!

Ah! then the lass that charms my eye,
The lass so simple, sweet and shy,
Had not been here, a wand'rer by
    The waters of the Concord;
She had not left her magic here,
A glamour in this atmosphere,
Nor looking once on them, made dear
    The waters of the Concord.

AMONG THE DAISIES.

Oh, has she forgotten that sweet summer day
When roving together we paused by the way
   And I decked her with daisies and kissed her?

How often since then when, with thoughts all my
    own,
By sunshiny fields I have wandered alone,
   I have looked on the daisies and missed her!

A presence that nothing of grace was denied,
A tall, slender figure, she stood at my side,
   With the light of my love falling o'er her.

How large were her eyes as on me they looked
    down!
How long were their lashes! How glossy and brown!
   There was none to be chosen before her.

How glinted the sun through her hat's rim of lace
And mingled its kisses with mine on her face!
   It is sad to be roving without her.

Ah, welladay! welladay! if it can be
That she has no thought of that sweet day or me
   When the fields are all daisies about her.

WE WERE PLAYMATES.

Come, sit beside my fire with me!—
A quarter of a century
Has passed since we together sat,
Dear lips say, on the chimney mat
And watched the evening fire until
The sandman came our eyes to fill.
A quarter of a century—
How much this means to you and me!
To those whose love still helps us bear
Our daily burden, daily care,
But for whose words we might not know
That we were playmates long ago!

Come, sit beside the fire with me!
And let us fancy it to be
The self-same fire that filled our eyes
With childish wonder and surprise,
And watch it till we seem to hear
The same old sandman drawing near!
Forget this evening—for we can—
The sober woman, serious man;

Revive, in all their simple joy,
The laughing girl and careless boy ;
That we may feel what others know —
That we were playmates long ago!

SONNETS.

MY FATHER.

This is my consolation: though no more
  As in remembered summers I shall be
  Among these hills with him, I feel that he,
Who knew them long and in his bosom bore
Great love for them, will seek them o'er and o'er
  And oft among them bear me company,
  So much of his clear vision giving me
That I shall find more beauty than before
In yonder purple mountains, yonder lake
  Now golden in the sunset, and, hard by,
    The woods that whisper, Peace! Beloved
        spirit!
He did not all the beauty here forsake;
  From what is fair on earth men do not die —
  'T is part of what in heaven they inherit.

TO ADDIE FRANCES SHAW.

My sister, my dear sister, gone before,
   Across the river, — that mysterious tide
   That flows between us, shadowy and wide,
Which I myself must soon or late pass o'er, —
I send you greeting, wishing you once more
   A happy birthday where you now reside
   Forgetting not the home from which you died,
Forgetting not the love for you I bore.
Now once again the violets have come
   And all the air is full of melody;
      The day is like your latest birthday here:
I weep not, for I feel about your home
   Beyond the river fairer flowers be
      And sweeter songs delight your listening ear.

FIRST SPEECH.

First speech is like the sudden blossoming
  Of trees, itself the blossoming of thought,
  As sudden: truth to us this morning brought,
When our dear daughter, three years old this spring,
In words well-chosen spake full many a thing
  Which late as yester morning we would not
  Have said that she could utter if not taught
By having it repeated, as birds sing
Their songs — without the slightest variance —
  Over again to her.   How suddenly
    Has she become a sweeter spray to us!
With what surprise to our delighted sense! —
  Her speech has come with subtile fragrancy,
    And in a way that seems miraculous.

APRIL 26, 1895.

I cannot think it is in mockery
  Of my sad looks that Nature smiles to-day;
  I cannot turn my face from hers away,
Because in hers no sign of grief I see.
To mourn is vain: not so to hope can be,
  And she would have me hope and hope alway;
  So my cold hand in her warm hand I lay;
She, mother-heart, knows what is best for me.
'T is well for me to hear the song she sings,
  To see the look, the radiant look, she wears:
  The hope in her does hope in me beget.
Tears solace somewhat, but are idle things
  Beyond a certain measure; and ill-fares
  The life that fosters nothing but regret.

TO BENJAMIN F. LEGGETT.

ON READING "A SHEAF OF SONG."

Leggett! your verse is beautiful to me,
  Because to me the simple and sincere
  Are beautiful. To you, who do not fear
To trust your thought, however fine it be,
Whatever its originality,
  To simple forms and words we daily hear;
  To you, who would not if you could appear
To feel more than you do feel,—gratefully
All lovers of the natural in art
  Should give applause: the time will come again
  For a return to that; and such as you,
Who, on the sleeve, prefer to wear the heart
  And in its forms and language speak to men,
  Are doing more than it was thought to do.

TO PASTOR FELIX.

I am with thee, though in this distant mart;
   I joy with thee, that she thou hold'st so dear
   Now lies so easy that the heavy fear
No longer with its burden bows thy heart.
I thank our God, whose servitor thou art,
   That thou no longer through the bitter tear
   In dark foreboding seest thy home appear
As in the shadow that no light can part.
Oh, my dear friend! thy vigils have been long,
   And thou hast need of quiet and repose;
      Now mayst thou sleep, and thus thy strength
         regain!
Rest thee awhile! and then in thy sweet song,
   Which, as a brook in leafy summer, flows,
      Make unto her thy bosom still more plain!

MISCELLANEOUS.

THE STOPPING OF THE STAGE.

At last our weary senses know
    How quiet are these summer hills;
Our horses, reeking long ago,
Now pause to drink where, cool and low,
    The wayside brook its fountain fills.

O grateful pause! wherein we see
    No changing in the landscape round,
No shifting of its scenery :
What restful immobility
    The eye has in all objects found!

O grateful pause! wherein we hear,
    In calm expansion over all,
The whisper of the pinewood near,
And, lightly to the listening ear,
    The brook among its pebbles fall.

But now each horse has drunk, and he
    Whose looks but one desire reveal
Climbs to his seat, and soon we see
The shifting of the scenery
    And only hear the rumbling wheel.

FROM THE HILL.

I left the noisy stage at noon,
  There at the thorp, two leagues away ;
  And, though it was a garish day
And I could not arrive too soon,
  Walked hither, for the simple sake
  Of the delight that I should take
In passing through the quaint old town
  Without the noise of wheel or hoof;
  Such quiet lay on every roof
On which this shaggy crest looked down.

The stage went on apace, and soon
  Its heavy rumble died away,
  And there was naught to rouse the day
From its repose of hollow noon
  Save, now and then, the sudden caw
  Of some bold crow and, though I saw
Nor bird nor perch, the tinkling song
  Of some shy thrush.   It seemed as though
  It were a charmèd town, and so
With noiseless feet I walked along.

Two leagues, by many a house and barn,
  By many a window, many a door,
  By many a sunlit threshing-floor
Wind-swept as is an open tarn,
  I came, and till I reached this spot
  No human form my glances caught;
No one was at the wayside well,
  At any window, door or gate;
  The town to me was desolate,
And silent as a silent bell.

And now I look o'er it, who see
  The long white way by which I came,
  The way I Via Pacis name,
And beautiful it is to me;
  Brown, shadowed homes in many a row,
  A picture softly etched below.
No sound from it can reach my ear;
  It will remain a charmèd town
  So long as o'er it I look down
From all the peace and quiet here.

LUXURIES.

Again I walk these woodland ways,
   A noisy season after;
Again I feel their cool and calm,
   And hear their leafy laughter.

In town, the idle luxurist
   On his divan is lying:
My senses here have luxuries
   The best of his outvying.

Better than horticultural growths
   That sicken in their vases,
These simple wilding flowers that lend
   These winding ways their graces.

Better than some exotic song
   From lips of languor falling,
The singing of these pebbly brooks
   And birds above me calling.

My luxuries not only please
   But strengthen with their beauty:
With lighter step I turn from them
   To labor and to duty.

TWO NATURE LOVERS.

If they were here, among these hills, with me,
Then perfect here would my contentment be ;
I long to-day for their society.

How much to me their absence has denied!
O, that they could have laid their oars aside
And left awhile their galley to the tide!

I know their love of nature equals mine;
I know they see in nature a design
To raise us up to that which is divine.

I know they hold that God with wise intent
Created all, o'er which well-pleased He bent,—
That beauty is no simple accident;

That unto them of quickened ear and eye,
It does His love and goodness testify :
How dull the sense that does this creed deny!

And so I would that they were here to-day,
To walk with me this winding, mossy way,
Wherein alone my noiseless feet delay,

Assured that theirs would be the peace that fills,
On this fair day, the voices of these rills
And all the gentle whispers of these hills.

But some may from the tasks assigned them, rest
While others must be doing His behest—
Come, sweet content! I know His will is best.

OUR LOVED ONES.

What gentle ones have passed away
    Since last we tarried here,
To whom these hills in their array
    Of summer leaves were dear,
To whom these woods were beautiful,
To whom these rills were musical,
    For many and many a year ! —
We look, we listen ; but too far
For word or sign our loved ones are !

What shadows in this sunlight fall
    By not an object cast ! —
Projections of the mind when all
    Its thoughts are of the past.
The bird that sings above our way
Is singing of a bygone day,
    And all that charmed the last
Sweet ramble of our loved ones here
Comes sadly to our eye and ear.

65

Oh, that they could return again
  As in the olden days,
Like pilgrims from the haunts of men
  To these sequestered ways,
Who felt, amid the beauty here,
That heaven must be very near,
  Just hidden from our gaze!
Oh, that our mournful voices might
Recall them to our longing sight!

But should we wish them here? Have they
  Not fairer scenes than these?
Reach not the heavenly hills away
  Through deeper silences?
Are not the woods of heaven more calm?
Have not the airs of heaven more balm,
  And softer melodies?—
Have they not found, in full release,
Eternal sunshine, rest, and peace?

TO A BOY.

Would Ben be dear to Nature, he
Must quiet in her presence be.

To such as come with careless rout
She does not pour her treasures out.

To such as ne'er her peace molest
She gives, and freely gives, her best.

She loves her lover all his days;
She loves him for his quiet ways.

She has for his quick eye and ear
What none beside may see or hear.

In gifts that charm his every sense
She shares with him her affluence.

So Ben will learn among these hills,
Beside these long-familiar rills,

To quiet in her presence live
That she to him her best may give;

That he may feel that he is dear
To her great heart that throbs so near.

67

UNTENANTED.

The lake is calm below;
　The hills are calm around;
The sighs of pines, that come and go,
　Are here the only sound.

For silent are the sheep
　That near me huddled lie,
As silent as the clouds that sleep
　Amid the stiller sky.

The quietude becomes
　So sad about the door,
It seems the hush of mourning homes
　Lies still the threshold o'er.

My step be lighter near!
　Uncovered be my head!
And let me with the pines I hear
　Be thoughtful of the dead!

LAKE SQUAM.

Squam is very fair to see
  When it lies at rest;
But it must forbidding be
When the winds disturbingly
  Fall upon its breast.

On a gentle summer day,
  I beheld its charms;
O, how peacefully it lay,
Smiling in the noontide ray
  And the forest's arms!

There was nothing anywhere
  To disturb the hush
That was deepened, here and there,
By a whispering woodland air
  Or a singing thrush.

If its legend — has it none? —
  Was inspired when it
Lay so quiet in the sun,
Then its legend must be one
  For a child's ear fit.

69

But if when some headlong air
  Broke its mirror bright
And its couch became a lair,
Rose its legend, then beware,
  For that must affright.

MY LADY BIRCH.

The birch, most shy and ladylike of trees.
— *Lowell.*

You are indeed a lady,
   My tall and slender birch;
And none will find a fairer one
   Wherever he may search.

My lady birch, I wonder
   What does my presence give
To one so very delicate,
   So finely sensitive.

I only know there never
   Seem darker stains on me
Than when I come and look on you
   And all your whiteness see.

My lady birch, I love you: —
   And yet, can love be right?
You are so very chaste and fair,
   So fitly veiled in white;

You look so like a spirit
   Beneath the moon and sun;
You are so purely beautiful; —
   A lady, wholly one.

71

IMPRESSIONS OF SUNSET.

I long to see among the hills again
The splendors I have seen.   There sunset seems
In peace and hush, as I have seen it oft,
To give to me some glimpses of that world,—
Its banded vales and mountains glorified,—
We feel is round us when our souls are moved;
To make it less a mystery and more near
Than we have felt, and to surround the world
Wherein we live, like a pure atmosphere.
And so I long among the hills again
To see what I have seen,—the sunset glimpse
Of what awaits me near, which I shall gain
By stepping little further into life,
As one who leaves the vale in shadow, finds
The hills above it overflown with light.

THE BONNY DOON.

I paused beside the Bonny Doon
  At midnight and alone,
And heard it tell the listening moon,
  In saddest undertone,
  The loss and sorrow by it known.

"What though in spring my birks grow sweet,
  In summer, shade my tide;
What though the years unchanged repeat
  Their magic at my side,—
No more to me the bard returns
  Who sang my banks and braes;
No more the lips of Robert Burns
  Are vocal in my praise."

"Oh, bonny Doon!" said I, "take heart,
  And learn this truth of me:
Immortal as his heavenly art
  The bard himself must be.
Though never to your banks and braes
  His wandering step returns,
The sweetest singer in your praise
  Is still your Robert Burns."

Yet, as before, beside the Doon,
  At midnight and alone,
I heard it tell the listening moon,
  In saddest undertone,
  The loss and sorrow by it known.

AT THE TOWER OF FONTENAY.

A voice comes out of the past to me,
  As I pause by these silent walls,
What time on them in solemnity
  The hush of the sunset falls;
And in that voice that is soft and low
  Is the pathos of love alway;
It tells of Anne of the long ago,
  And the Tower of Fontenay.

Ah! then it is that each gentle air,
  As it wanders these ruins by,
Kisses the walls and the vines they bear
  And departs with its saddest sigh;
Ah! then it is turns the winding Loire
  With its tenderest look away;
And mine the thoughts of all nature are
  By the Tower of Fontenay.

I hear her sing, and I see her dance;
  I behold her bewitching charms,

That won for her in the court of France
The reception of open arms;
But oh! a grief in my heart is born,
As I think of that fateful day
When she was borne to that court at morn
From the Tower of Fontenay.

And ever the voice that is heard by me,
As I pause by these silent walls,
What time on them in solemnity
The hush of the sunset falls,
Whispers the wish that is in my heart—
And the wish will be there alway—
That she had dwelt from the world apart
At the Tower of Fontenay.

[At the Tower of Fontenay the beautiful and unfortu-
nate Anne Boleyn " grew up with the children of her host
* * * and was the favorite and delight of all. * * * She
danced with a grace that made her a little wonder to those
who crowded to see her execute the intricate figures of the
day with her cousins, who endeavored, without envy, to
emulate her acquirements. Her voice possessed remarka-
ble sweetness and a pathos that was peculiarly attractive.
Even at a very early age it had a charm that troubled all
hearts."]

ASHHURST — A HOME.

Ashhurst has a restful quiet,
  And I seek it oft;
Few the feet that e'er pass by it,
  And their tread is soft; —
Shadows of the ash-trees tall
On its mossy dooryard fall.

Ashhurst has a cosey study
  Just above its door;
You may see the windows ruddy
  Ere the day is o'er,
When the thrush is in the wood
And the west is rosy-hued.

Ashhurst has a singer living
  In its pleasant shade;
One to whom is Nature giving
  Evermore her aid;
Simple is the life he leads —
Few his wants as are his needs.

77

Ashhurst, it is vocal ever
  With his tuneful words,
Sung so easily that never
  More so sing the birds;
All its leafy dooryard trees
Catch his airy melodies.

Ashhurst for me ever gladly
  Hangs its latchstring out;
May I never come and sadly
  Looking all about,
Find no latchstring in the door
And a shadow all things o'er!

THE WAYSIDE ELMS.

A leafy luxury.— *Keats.*

When pass I to and fro the mill,
  Amid the noon of day,
When dull with haze lies every hill
  Seen southward from my way,—
How pleasant are these elms that throw
  Their shadows over me!
They give, beneath the sunny glow,
  A leafy luxury.

The weaver longs her loom beside,
  The smith his anvil o'er,
To tarry by some wood-rimmed tide,
  In paths of moss, once more.
Who doubts that they, in passing here,
  Forget awhile their lot,—
Too grateful for what good is near
  To sigh for what is not?

79

Though here is not the breath of balm,
   The lapse of idle lin,
I something feel of cool and calm
   These airy shadows in.
Blow, wind of summer, lightly blow
   The branches over me! —
How wood-like in the noonday glow
   Becomes a single tree!

A MOMENT OF SUNSHINE.

The sunshine at this moment falls
So brightly on my study walls,

They seem to have been wrought of gold,
Like those of Incan palace old.

I lay my toiling stylus by —
No Inca was more rich than I.

I sit, like him, in golden shine,
And all his splendid state is mine;

I look on walls all gorgeous, rich
With leaf-wrought arch and statued niche,

And gazing from my windows, see
Gardens of gold surrounding me.

I have, like him, a wealth untold,
My birthright in a " Place of Gold."

———————

O bright illusion! leaving me
The dull, the dim, the shadowy ;

No leaf-wrought arch, no statued niche,
No walls, no gardens, gorgeous, rich ;

But, humbler now than e'er before,
Surroundings that may please no more.

I take my stylus up anew,
And like a drudge my task pursue ;

But I have known what 't is to sit
In splendor for a monarch fit ;

To be as rich as any one
Of the "descendants of the sun,"

A moment,— but that moment seemed
Life-long, as if I had but dreamed.

THE DANDELION.

Though 't is praised by many a poet,
By its homely name I know it;
Though its garment is so gay,
It will always seem to me
Living in a humble way;
For, with real humility,
It would come and sit of yore
Just beside my kitchen-door.

I am minded once again
Of the simple fact that then
None of all the other flowers
In the dooryard seemed to me,
Who would pass with them long hours,
So familiar — if that be
Just the word — with each and all
Of that household I recall.

Yes, familiar, if I say,
In an unobtrusive way.
It was welcome when it came;
For it sat beside the door,
Like a ruddy, round-faced dame,
To be social — nothing more:
Not for gossip, for its heart
Was too warm for such a part.

I have learned since then how wide
Is its home — by riverside,
Over hill and thorough vale,
On the highway, in the lane,
Almost everywhere — and pale
Grow the colors — shown in vain —
Worn by others when they dare
With its garment theirs compare.

Still, though queenly it may sit
To some minds observing it,
It will always seem to me,
Though 't is met in divers ways,
Of the same humility
That it was in early days,
When it came and kindly-eyed
Sat my kitchen-door beside.

WE COME TO GIVE THESE LITTLE CHILDREN.

(READ BY GEO. W. BICKNELL, D. D.,
CHILDREN'S SUNDAY.)

We come not, Lord, before Thine altar,
    For newer tokens of Thy love;
For fresher waters from Thy fountains,
    And blossoms from Thy fields above.

We need not more than Thou hast given
    Whereby Thy boundless good to see —
We come, O Lord! to make apparent
    The fulness of our trust in Thee.

We come to give these little children
    Of whom Thy tender love is told;
Remembering how came the mothers
    With children in the days of old.

Ah! they are more than birds and sunbeams
    That fill our homes with song and light, —
The sweetness of whose tender presence
    Is round us in the day and night.

85

We give them, Lord, that in Thy bosom
  The budding of their years may be;
And wilt Thou take them, as we give them,
  A token of our trust in Thee?

IN MEMORIAM:

J. B.

JANUARY 23, 1897.

I sat in a house of mourning
  On the open side of a hill,
And I heard the pastor saying
  What my eyes with tears did fill.

'T was a pure, white day in winter,
  And the man that there lay dead
Had fallen beneath his burden
  With an aureole round his head.

And as I bowed and listened,
  The voice of the wind I heard,
That sighed and moaned, nay, that uttered
  Full many a sorrowful word.

I cannot tell which touched me
  The deeper or said the more,—
The plaintive voice in my presence,
  Or that at each window and door.

87

But I shall always remember
How Nature lamented the loss
Of one that had learned her patience
And in silence borne his cross.

' THE AFTERTHOUGHT.

My little boy had sought my room where I
  Was busy with my books;
I saw the light that kindled in his eye,
  I saw his roguish looks.

I knew what he had come for, and I knew —
  Who kissed his forehead fair—
I could not well my quiet task pursue
  With him at frolic there.

But I was loth to bid him run away,
  His little playmates find,
Till books and papers in confusion lay
  Before me and behind.

Then in my hand I took his hand and led
  Him silent to the door,
And yielding to the moment's impulse said,—
  " You must come here no more."

He went away, with a reluctant look
   That I remember well;
Soon after, when I had resumed my book,
   Its leaves to ashes fell.

The fancy that had pleased me passed away,
   Ere it in words was caught;
And heavily upon my bosom lay
   The burden of a thought.

What if my boy should seek my room no more?
   What if I should not see
Him cast again his baubles on its floor
   To play at peep with me?

Oh, what were then the stillness of my room
   And all the house beside?—
Would I not wish that I had bade him come
   Or I with him had died?

THE FARMER'S DAUGHTER.

Yes, they tell the truth who say
  She 's the flower of the town;
I — I saw her yesterday
  When the sun was going down,
    Milk the kie
    While I stood by,
In the barn beside the way.

She is graceful, lithe, and tall,
  And her fair looks are more fair
Since you find she is of all,
  All her beauty unaware;
    She has not
    Of self a thought
That you would not modest call.

It was a delight to see
  One so lovely, one so fair,
Give herself ungrudgingly
  To such unbefitting care;
    But the charms
    Of her bare arms
Were not known except to me.

Shall I tell her how she looks?
  What might be her walk in life?—
Here, where flow the crystal brooks,
  Where the gifts of God are rife,
    She has found
    That joys abound,—
Views are pictures, flowers are books.

Here, these simple lives among,
  She has kept her native ways;
Pure in heart, forever young,
  She has lived contented days:
    In her ears
    For eighteen years,
Thrush and bobolink have sung.

Shall she now herself behold
  In some polished poet's song?—
Better in some fountain cold
  Which the rushes grow along.
    Better far
    Her sweet looks are
That of them she is not told.

Still, I cannot help the thought
  How in urban church and hall
By her beauty would be caught

The admiring eyes of all;
    Nor how much
    For its soft touch
Would her dimpled hand be sought.

It may be I am in love;
    I am willing to confess
Sentiment that is above
    What is common tenderness;
        That I feel
        What few conceal —
More than does mere liking prove.

A SUMMER INCIDENT.

She had a fine and delicate,
  A quick, imaginative mind,
And she was tall and fair, with all
  The graces of young womankind.

She stood before me, wonder-eyed,
  With looks that now my mem'ry haunt,
While her gray sailor uncle told
  The story of the corposant.

So graphic were his gestured words,
  She walked the windy deck at night
And saw the fiery meteor hang
  On yard and spar its ball of light.

To her, as to the scared that quit
  The King's ship for the foaming sea,
The meteor was an imp of hell
  That played its pranks most frightfully.

94

I saw her large eyes larger grow
    As more and more grew her dismay;
I wished to lead her, gentle-voiced,
    From what seemed all too real away;

To speak such words of tenderness
    As might discover something more;
But other ears and eyes than hers,
    How vain they made the wish I bore!

THE COUNTRY STAGE DRIVER.

You cannot find a man to-day
More hearty in his word or way
Than he who drove, some years ago,
The village-rousing tallyho.

I mean the typic driver, who
The straight way to your good will knew;
Who cracked his whip and cracked his joke,
And called by name the country folk;

Who told you more in one short ride,
If you and he sat side by side,
Than half a dozen men could tell,
Or you could e'er remember well;

Who knew each home his long route passed,
Its history, from first to last,
If it had ups and downs in life,
If shirked the man or worked the wife;

Who taught a moral, told a tale
And much that turned a red cheek pale;
Was doctor, lawyer, prophet too,
For he could say what all should do.

I miss him here among these hills
Whose circuit now his memory fills,
Where, pressed against his burly side,
I felt his strong pulse through the ride.

Big, honest fellow, with a grasp
That held your hand as in a clasp,—
Recalling faces scarcely seen,
And keeping many a memory green,—

Peace, peace to him! who, four-in-hand,
Did not his team alone command,
But, cheery-voiced, as you may know,
Each genial heart on his tallyho.

JOE OF KATAHDIN.

When winds of winter fiercely blow
O'er dreary wastes of sleet and snow,
Then comes to me the thought of Joe,
    Whose home is near Katahdin.
'T is always an inspiring thought;
For though most humble is his lot,
He stands 'mong men as high, I wot,
    As stands 'mong hills Katahdin.

I know him as a man sincere,
Whose mind has been for many a year
Uplifted by his living near
    And gazing on Katahdin;
Right in his ample brow — to me
As rugged as his hill's — I see
His measure of nobility
    Impressive as Katahdin.

No rougher hands than his are felt;
But what a heart through them does melt!
He nobly wears his leather belt
    As wears its spruce Katahdin.
I see him now, and on his breast
By no religious doubt deprest,
His beard, in wintry whiteness, rest,
    Like snow-drifts on Katahdin.

But he is poor as he is old ;
And now that wild winds, bleak and cold,
Are blowing 'round his trembling fold
    Down o'er which looks Katahdin,
I, who have known in summer days
His kind and hospitable ways,
Should gild his hours with genial rays
    Like sunshine on Katahdin.

And so with this poor bit of rhyme,
I send him, mindful of the time,
The rigor of his northern clime
    That caps with snow Katahdin,
What shall give warmth to him afield
And comfort by his fireside yield:
My heart to him is not congealed
    When ices block Katahdin.

BURNS.

His right to a place among the greatest poets in Europe being no longer in dispute, to speak of him still as the Ayrshire Bard is almost as dull an affectation as to follow his own example and call him Rob, or Robin.—*John Service.*

Now no more the Bard of Ayrshire—
  Once a better name denied—
Whom the lords of Edinboro'
  Thought to humble at their side;
But the sweetest of all singers
  That the world has ever known,
With a fame for which those nobles,
  Could they now, would give their own.

Now no more the Bard of Ayrshire,
  But the poet of the heart,
In whose songs of love and pathos
  Nature leaves no room for art;
Who has shown the lowly peasant
  Has as fine an eye and ear,
Has as keen a sense of beauty,
  As the wigged and powdered peer.

Now no more the Bard of Ayrshire,
  But the sharp-tongued satirist,
Shaming now the titled idler,
  Now the pulpit dogmatist;
Hating pride, with honest hatred,
  Cant and all hypocrisy;
Hating caste and holding manhood
  As the sole nobility.

Now no more the Bard of Ayrshire,
  But the poet dear to all
That regard the tenant only,
  Not his cottage or his hall:
Loving justice, life is better
  Since his tuneful work began;
For 't is God-like to consider
  Not the raiment but the man.

WISE AND TESTY.

I had some converse the other day
With that old blacksmith across the way.

"Or sledge or anvil a man must be,
For none can be both," he said to me.

And then he hammered a little bit,
And paused to see how I looked at it.

I saw the wisdom that I should own;
But bent on mischief, and that alone,

I begged to differ and said, " 'T is true
Some men are anvils and sledges too;

Sledges at home and anvils away,
Pounding and pounded, they live their day."

I struck the iron when it was hot,
And I was sure of the fun I sought;

But soon the sparks flew so thick and fast
That we were both all ablaze at last.

Pounding and pounded, no man could say
Which was the anvil or sledge that day.

And when we parted, it seemed to me
That we had lost all our dignity.

The words that vexed us, may God forgive!—
I did not know I was sensitive.

You laugh; but mark! it is time ill-spent
To argue merely for argument.

JOHN SHAW—1738.

John Shaw, the English taverner,
  Who liked not hours late,
Would bid all folk begone from his tavern,
  And put up his shutters, at eight.

No matter who the folk were,
  If they were high or low,
He snapped his whip o'er all who tarried
  Till they were fain to go.

But better the punch he vended
  Than that of other men,
And many who left him in passion
  Came back to his punch again.

So good were the limes he usèd,
  So good was the pine-apple rum,
He needed no bush for his tavern—
  The pennies were sure to come.

Now one who was a law-maker
Was of this taverner told,
And he wished to taste, for he was a bibler,
The famous punch he sold.

He took his friends to the tavern:
Uncommon folk were they;
But as soon as eight by the old town-clock
They were bade to haste away.

"Oh! urge it not, mine host, I beg you,"
The wise law-maker cried,
" And do in the case of certain persons
Some certain laws provide!"

Outspake the loud-voiced taverner,
For a man of courage was he,
" My good sir, you are a law-maker
And should not a law-breaker be.

"If you and all others, I give you warning,
Leave not forthwith this room,
You will go from it as sorry and wet-shod
As ever you went to your home.

"For my good old servant, Molly,
    With her mop and bucket waits near: —
He comes to be off while he is sober
    Whoever it is comes here."

As rude to us as may seem the outward,
    The inward was good indeed: '
How often in life have we censured the manner,
    For we knew not of the need!

Are we not moved, as the wives who thanked him,
    To weave his name with these flowers:
Praise for the courage that never failed him!
    And praise for his early hours!

[John Shaw opened a tavern in the Old Shambles, Manchester, in 1738, and began at once to close it at eight o'clock in the evening, and if any persons tarried after this hour, the methods of ejectment were as stated in the lines. He was heartily thanked by the women folks for so rigorously carrying out his regulation as to the hour of closing, and so popular did he become among the men folks that a club known as the John Shaw Club was formed, of which he was chosen president, which existed up to 1860, and may be, for all I know, in existence now. He set a good example, and I think his memory is entitled to the tribute I pay it. If my lines are not " pointed with a moral," I think they will suggest one to every reader.]